Thematic Poetry

All About Me!

**More Than 30 Perfect Poems with Instant Activities to Enrich
Your Lessons, Build Literacy, and Celebrate the Joy of Poetry**

by Betsy Franco and Friends

SCHOLASTIC
PROFESSIONAL BOOKS

New York • Toronto • London • Auckland • Sydney • Mexico City • New Delhi • Hong Kong

For Maria Damon,
who gives me confidence in my poetry

I would especially like to thank Bobbi Katz, Sandra Liatsos, and Leslie Danford Perkins who helped make this collection come alive. I am also very grateful for Liza Charlesworth, my wonderful editor.

ACKNOWLEDGMENTS

ARNOLD ADOFF. "INside" from OUTSIDE INSIDE POEMS by Arnold Adoff. Text copyright © 1981 by Arnold Adoff. By permission of Lothrop, Lee & Shepard Books, a division of William Morrow & Company, Inc.

ALBERTO FORCADA. "Belly Button" from DESPERTAR (TO WAKE UP) by Alberto Forcada. Published by CIDCLI, Centro de Informacion y Desarrollo de la Comunicacion y la Literatura Infantiles, from Mexico City.

KARAMA FUFUKA. "Basketball Star" from MY DADDY IS A COOL DUDE AND OTHER POEMS by Karama Fufuka. Copyright © 1975 by Karama Fufuka. Used by permission of Dial Books for Young Readers, a division of Penguin Putnam Inc.

NIKKI GIOVANNI. "the drum" and "two friends" from SPIN A SOFT BLACK SONG by Nikki Giovanni. Copyright © 1971, 1985 by Nikki Giovanni. Reprinted by permission of Farrar, Straus & Giroux, Inc.

MARY ANN HOBERMAN. "Shy" and "Sometimes" from FATHERS, MOTHERS, SISTERS, BROTHERS by Mary Ann Hoberman. Copyright © 1991 by Mary Ann Hoberman. By permission of Little, Brown and Company. "Birthdays" from THE LLAMA WHO HAD NO PAJAMA: 100 FAVORITE POEMS by Mary Ann Hoberman. Copyright © 1981 by Mary Ann Hoberman. Reprinted by permission of Harcourt Brace & Company.

FELICE HOLMAN. "Sulk" from I HEAR YOU SMILING AND OTHER POEMS by Felice Holman. Copyright © 1973 by Felice Holman. Reprinted by permission of the author. Published by Charles Scribner's Sons.

LEE BENNETT HOPKINS. "Digging for Treasure" from CHARLIE'S WORLD by Lee Bennett Hopkins. Copyright © 1972 Lee Bennett Hopkins. Originally published by Bobbs Merrill. "This Tooth" from ME! by Lee Bennett Hopkins. Copyright © 1970 Lee Bennett Hopkins. Originally published by Seabury Press. Both are reprinted by permission of Curtis Brown, Ltd.

LANGSTON HUGHES. Excerpt from BLACK MISERY by Langston Hughes. Copyright Text © 1969 by Arna Bontemps and George Houston Bass as Executors of the Estate of Langston Hughes. Used by permission of Oxford University Press, Inc.

BOBBI KATZ. "Skin" and "Sing Song" by Bobbi Katz. "Skin" copyright © 1978 Bobbi Katz; "Sing Song" copyright © 1981 by Bobbi Katz. Both are reprinted by permission of the author.

SANDRA LIATSOS. "My First Birthday Gift" by Sandra Liatsos. Copyright © 1991 by Sandra Liatsos. Used by permission of Marian Reiner for the author.

EVE MERRIAM. "Wishing" and "A Matter of Taste" from THERE IS NO RHYME FOR SILVER by Eve Merriam. Copyright © 1962, 1990 Eve Merriam. Used by permission of Marian Reiner.

LESLIE DANFORD PERKINS. "Moonlight" by Leslie Danford Perkins. Copyright © 2000 by Leslie Danford Perkins. Used by permission of the author who controls all rights.

Cover design by Norma Ortiz
Interior design by Ellen Matlach Hassell
for Boultinghouse & Boultinghouse, Inc.
Illustrations by James Graham Hale
Copyright © 2000 by Betsy Franco
ISBN: 0-439-09848-3
Printed in the U.S.A.

Contents

Introduction

This collection of poems and the other collections in this series will come in very handy as you dive into your yearly themes. The poetry in *All About Me!* has been thoughtfully written and compiled with preschool to second grade children clearly in mind. Variety, usability, and fun topped the list of considerations in selecting or creating each and every poem.

There are so many ways the poems can be used, so why not get the most you can from each one? Whether you present a poem a week or a poem a day, you can dip into this collection with confidence. Use the poems in coordination with your phonics program. You can read aloud the poems, transfer them to a pocket chart, and then let children act them out. In addition, the collection provides jumping off points for writing and fits into the math, science, and social studies curricula.

Phonemic Elements

Phonics and poetry go hand in hand. For instance, look at the rhyming words in the poem "Skin" (page 7)—*in, skin; fit, it*. Transfer this ten-line poem to a pocket chart and then highlight the rhyming words. This can lead nicely into other activities that focus on the short-*i* sound.

In a similar way, "Sulk" (page 28) works well for the short-vowel sound, and "A Matter of Taste" (page 19) is tailor-made for focusing on the digraphs *ch* and *sh* (*crunchy, cheese, chewy, marshmallow*).

Some poems naturally lend themselves to consonant study. "If I Had a Kingdom" (page 31) has several words that begin with the letter *k*, while "Things That Are Easy" (page 27) has lots of alliteration, such as "bounce a big red rubber ball." Introduce the poem "This Tooth" (page 26) to your class to have fun with the letter *j*.

Being Authors and Illustrators

Predictable language in poetry can make children feel confident about their own reading and writing. Help children anticipate the rhyming words or repeated phrases in the poems. Then encourage them to go one more step by making up new verses, or poems on similar themes or in similar formats. For instance, after reading the traditional song "If You're Happy and You Know It" (page 24), children can write new verses about snapping their fingers, stamping their feet, and so on.

When a poem looks like what it's saying, as "Moonlight" (page 25) and "My Extra-Special Box" (page 25) do, it is called a visual or concrete poem. Another example is "My Moves" (page 16), in which the lines are formatted to fit their meanings. Children can make their own visual poetry about their own extra-special boxes or some moves they like to make.

A poem such as "I'm Special, You're Special" (page 6) can be copied on a page with appropriate blanks for children to complete, as shown below. Let children complete this activity individually or as a class.

> You could travel from _____
> to Tennessee,
> and you'd never find someone
> who _____ like me.

Some poems ask questions. "What I'm Sposed to Do" (page 20) asks children if they know what they'd like to be when they grow up. "What's Cool at School?" (page 18) questions them about favorite school subjects, while "A Matter of Taste" (page 19) asks about their taste in food. These poems invite children to engage in writing (or dictating).

Why not take a poem and make it into a little foldable book, with one line per page? Children can illustrate each page, making the poem more personal and, subsequently, more meaningful. A class collaborative book can be similarly effective. "The First Time" (page 23) might spawn a book of memories about firsts in the children's lives, "My Pet Wish List" (page 17) can be a springboard for writing about pets that children wish for, and "If I Had a Kingdom" (page 31) can spark children's imaginations about a perfect world.

Reading and Acting Out Poetry

Poems provide delightful opportunities for dramatic play. Children can act out "My Moves" (page 16), or teach each other things based on "A Friendly Circle" (page 10). "If You're Happy and You Know It" (page 24) is also a natural vehicle for dramatic play.

Some poems can be adapted to a call-and-response format in which half the children say some of the lines or verses and the other half complete the lines or verses. You can use "Sing Song" (page 11) in this way. A poem such as "Talent Show" (page 15) works well in a Reader's Theater format—different lines can be assigned to different children, and they can act out the poem as well. You can even hold a real talent show in your classroom.

With many poems in the collection, it can be fun to emphasize the rhyme and rhythm as you read. Encourage children to clap, snap, or jump to the rhythm so they can feel the poems in their bodies.

Science, Math, and Social Studies Links

All About Me! focuses on self-esteem and feelings, relationships, tastes, and talents. Respect for self and others reverberates throughout the collection. For example, different kinds of families are highlighted in "Graphing Families" (page 12). Accepting feelings is the focus of "Feelings" (page 24), and the uniqueness of each child is the subject of "I'm Special, You're Special" (page 6).

Math opportunities abound as well. You can use the poem "Graphing Families" (page 12) as an introduction to making a graph of the number of people in the children's families. In a similar vein, "In the Middle" (page 14) sets up a nice graphing exercise about position in the family. After reading "A Matter of Taste" (page 19) and "My Pet Wish List" (page 17), children can make a people graph or a bar graph of their preferences and analyze the results.

Science comes up in the poem "Belly Button" (page 26), which might lead to a lesson on air and balloons.

The collection includes multicultural selections that help children appreciate diverse cultures. For example, "the drum" (page 8) by Nikki Giovanni and "Black Misery" (page 11) by Langston Hughes are both written by African American poets. "Belly Button" (page 26) by Alberto Forcada is written in both English and Spanish. Encourage children to bring in poems from their own cultures as a lovely extension to *All About Me!*

The Home Connection

Poetry always works well as a link to the home. Children can share the poems, their illustrations of the poems, or new verses the class wrote. Poetry is short and easy to read, and it has emotional power for both children and their families.

The treasures in *All About Me!* are yours for the taking. Take advantage of the curricular links, the phonetics, the reading and writing opportunities, and the multicultural aspects—but most of all, enjoy the poetry!

I'm Special, You're Special

You could search on the land
and search in the sea,
and you'd never find someone
exactly like me.

You could search from Hawaii
to Timbuktu,
and you'd never find someone
exactly like you.

You could travel from China
to Tennessee,
and no one would act
exactly like me.

You could check from Egypt
to Kalamazoo,
and no one would think
exactly like you.

For I am me and
you are you,
I am special and
you are, too.

Betsy Franco

Thematic Poems for the Classroom: All About Me! Scholastic Professional Books

Skin

The suit your body comes packed in
Is something magic called your skin.
It comes in every single shade
That anyone was ever made.
If someone's skin just did not fit
I never ever heard of it!
While summer shines and winter blows,
Your skin just grows and grows and grows
With all of you packed right inside—
A perfect place for bones to hide!

Bobbi Katz

the drum

daddy says the world is
a drum tight and hard
and i told him
i'm gonna beat
out my own rhythm

Nikki Giovanni

Which Me to Be

This morning I was late to school
and I can tell you why:
I changed my clothes
so many times—
I just could not decide.

I changed from plain to stripes and then
from blue to red to green.
I wouldn't, couldn't
make up my mind
about which me to be.

Betsy Franco

Thematic Poems for the Classroom: All About Me! Scholastic Professional Books

The More We Get Together

The more we get together,
together, together,
The more we get together,
the happier we'll be.
For your friends are my friends,
and my friends are your friends.
The more we get together,
the happier we'll be.

Author Unknown

A Friendly Circle

I taught Kim to build a castle
Kim taught Bo to finger wrestle,
Bo taught Trish to draw a pig.
Trish taught me to do a jig.

You and your friends
could do it, too.
Just teach them what
you love to do.

Betsy Franco

two friends

lydia and shirley have
two pierced ears and
two bare ones
five pigtails
two pairs of sneakers
two berets
two smiles
one necklace
one bracelet
lots of stripes and
one good friendship

Nikki Giovanni

Misery is when your
very best friend
calls you a name she really
didn't mean to call you at all.

Misery is when you call
your very best friend a name
you didn't mean to call her, either.

Langston Hughes

Making Friends

What's your name?
Would you like to play?
Come and join us.
What do you say?

Betsy Franco

Sing Song

I've got a new friend
A special me-and-you friend
A like-the-things-you-do friend
To play with every day!

I've got a new friend
A share-all-the-same-stuff friend
A never-be-too-tough friend
To play with *every* day!

Bobbi Katz

Graphing Families

In class we graphed our families
I counted five in mine—
my parents and my brother
and me and Grandpa Stein.

Some kids lived with their mamas,
Some kids lived with their dads.
Some kids lived with their grandmas
or their favorite granddads.

If we should make a graph again,
then mine'll change to seven,
for yesterday my mom had twins,
my brothers, Dan and Devon!

Betsy Franco

My First Birthday Gift

They didn't give me
a doll or book,
a stuffed giraffe
or game.
On the day
that I was born
my present was
my name!

Sandra Liatsos

Birthdays

If birthdays happened once a week
Instead of once a year,
Think of all the gifts you'd get
And all the songs you'd hear
And think of how quickly you'd grow up;
Wouldn't it feel queer
If birthdays happened once a week
Instead of once a year?

Mary Ann Hoberman

In the Middle (according to Terry)

My little brother tells on me,
My older sister teases.
My sister gets the privileges,
My bro does what he pleases.
If I could choose the place I'd be,
I wouldn't choose the middle.
I'd either be the biggest one
or else I would be little.

In the Middle (according to Chris)

My older bro sticks up for me,
My little sister's tough.
He taught me how to bat and pitch,
She shares her toys and stuff.
If I could choose the place to be,
I'd always choose the middle.
It's hard to be the biggest
and I've already been little.

Betsy Franco

Thematic Poems for the Classroom: All About Me! Scholastic Professional Books

Talent Show

We all showed off our talents
at the school talent show,
Each person's good at different things—
as if you didn't know.

Teresa read a funny poem,
and Tommy played the drums,
Rosita's good at magic tricks
and Mei-Mei really hums.

And as for me, I talk a lot—
now that's a real fact.
So I was the announcer who
announced each person's act!

Betsy Franco

My Moves

I can skip
and I can hop
and I can jump a rope.
I can tiptoe,
I can climb
and roll
      right down
          a slope

But when I'm late
I never skip,
I never jump or hop,
I never tiptoe, roll or climb.
I run as fast as my legs will go
to try to be on time!

Betsy Franco

Colors

Colors are pretty. Colors are fun.
Tell me. Which color's your favorite one?

Blue is the sky and blue is the sea.
Yellow's the stripes on a bumblebee.

Red is an apple; white is a blizzard.
Green is the back of a baby lizard.

Black and brown are the garden dirt.
Purple's the throat of a hummingbird.

Orange are the pumpkins out in the sun.
Tell me. Which color's your favorite one?

Betsy Franco

Thematic Poems for the Classroom: All About Me! Scholastic Professional Books

My Pet Wish List

I had a list of favorite pets
I hoped my mom would let me get—
a parrot and a kitty cat,
a kangaroo, a baby rat.

My mom said no to all of those
and to a billy goat and crow,
but mom will surely change her mind
when I bring home a buffalo!

Betsy Franco

Wishing

If I could have
Any wish that could be

I'd wish that a dog
Could have me.

Eve Merriam

What's Cool at School?

Reading
Writing
Math
P.E.
Social studies
Spelling bee
Which one
do you
think is
cool?
What's
your
favorite
thing
in school?

Betsy Franco

Playing at Recess

There's running and skipping
and hopping and jumping.

There's shooting and throwing
and kicking a ball.

There's climbing and hanging
and flipping and swinging.

Which one is the one that
you do best of all?

Betsy Franco

Thematic Poems for the Classroom: All About Me! Scholastic Professional Books

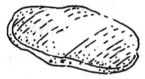

A Matter of Taste

What does your tongue like the most?
Chewy meat or crunchy toast?

A lumpy bumpy pickle or tickly pop?
A soft marshmallow or a hard lime drop?

Hot pancakes or a sherbet freeze?
Celery noise or quiet cheese?

Or do you like pizza
More than any of these?

Eve Merriam

What I'm Sposed to Do

When I'm grown up and need to work,
I don't know what I'll do.
I thought about the jobs I've seen,
and listed quite a few:

I could tend goats,
  mend coats,
   play notes,
    or sail boats.

I could make pots,
  give shots,
   write plots,
    or care for tots.

I could fix phones,
  mend bones,
   give loans,
    or polish stones.

My list is nice—I read it twice,
I still don't have a clue.
About the job I'd like the best,
And what I'm sposed to do.
Do you?

Betsy Franco

Thematic Poems for the Classroom: All About Me! Scholastic Professional Books

Basketball Star

When I get big
I want to be the best
basketball player in the world.
I'll make jumpshots, hookballs
and layups
and talk about dribble—
mine'll be outta sight!

Karama Fufuka

Thematic Poems for the Classroom: All About Me! Scholastic Professional Books

Which Animal?

If you could be an animal,
yes, any one at all,
Then you could have a neck so long
it made you very tall.

Or you could crawl like a crocodile
or jump like a kangaroo.
Perhaps you'd like to quack or chirp
or cock-a-doodle-doo?

Or would you like to grow two wings
and soar into the sky?
There're lots of insects you could be
like ants or butterflies?

You'd have a choice of sounds to make
and what you'd like to "wear"—
like feathers, scales and horns and shells
and plain or spotted hair.

Why, you could be a giant whale
or a teeny-tiny flea?
If you could be an animal,
which animal would you be?

Betsy Franco

Thematic Poems for the Classroom: All About Me! Scholastic Professional Books

The First Time

I remember the day I blew
my first bubble.
Before that great day it was
lots of trouble.

I remember the day I first
tied my shoe,
It took me a while because
it was new.

I remember the day I first
learned to cook,
but the best of my "firsts"
was reading a book!

Betsy Franco

Feelings

There's happy, embarrassed,
and silly and sad,
There's excited, delighted,
and frightened and glad.

I've had lots of feelings
already today.
And mom says it's only been
half of a day!

Betsy Franco

If You're Happy and You Know It

If you're happy and you know it,
clap your hands.
If you're happy and you know it,
clap your hands.
If you're happy and you know it,
then your life will surely show it.
If you're happy and you know it,
clap your hands.

Author Unknown

Thematic Poems for the Classroom: All About Me! Scholastic Professional Books

My Extra-Special Box

A tiny shell, a little
fox, a piece of wax
go in my box.
They're all mixed
up with beads and
rocks inside my
extra-special box.

Betsy Franco

Moonlight

On
  the
    dark
     lawn
      is a
      pale
      moon
     path
   just
  for
me

Leslie Danford Perkins

This Tooth

I jiggled it
   jaggled it
   jerked it.

I pushed
   and pulled
   and poked it.

But—

As soon as I stopped
and left it alone,
This tooth came out
on its very own!

Lee Bennett Hopkins

Belly Button

Like the balloons
that float at parties,
I have a knot on my belly
so I won't go flat.

Alberto Forcada
translated by Judith Infante

Ombligo

Como los globos
que flotan en las fiestas,
tengo, para no desinflarme,
un nudo en el estómago.

INside

the house is my room   and inside the room is my bed
and
inside
        the bed is
                me   under the covers
listening to the
        outside tree

Arnold Adoff

Things That Are Easy

It's easy to lift up my friend in a pool,
It's easy to daydream and doodle at school.

It's easy to slide on a floor in my socks,
It's easy to play in a big empty box.

It's easy to bounce a big red rubber ball,
It's easy to land in the leaves in the fall.

It's easy to giggle, it's easy to laugh,
It's easy to wrinkle when I'm in the bath!

Betsy Franco

Sulk

I scuff
   my feet along
And puff
   my lower lip
I sip my milk
   in slurps
And huff
And frown
And stamp around
And tip my chair
   back from the table
Nearly fall down
   but I don't care
I scuff
And puff
and frown
And huff
And stamp
And pout
Till I forget
What it's about

Felice Holman

Shy

Sometimes when I don't want to go
To visit someone I don't know,
They never stop to ask me why.
She's shy
They say
She's shy
Or if we're leaving someone's house,
They say I'm quiet as a mouse
When I forget to say good-bye.
She's shy
They say
She's shy
Cat's got her tongue, they always say,
She often does clam up this way,
She's silent as a stone today.
She's shy
They say
She's shy
I am not shy—or if I am
I'm not a mouse or stone or clam.
I like to look and listen to
What other people say and do.
If I can't think of things to say,
Why should I say things anyway?
I don't see why
That makes me shy

Mary Ann Hoberman

Thematic Poems for the Classroom: All About Me! Scholastic Professional Books

Digging for Treasure

I put my hand in
and found—

a rusty skate key,
a part of a tool,
a dead bee I was saving
to take into school;

my library card
and
a small model rocket.

I guess it is time
to clean out
my pocket.

Lee Bennett Hopkins

Thematic Poems for the Classroom: All About Me! Scholastic Professional Books

If I Had a Kingdom

If I had a kingdom
then I would be king.
Yes, I would be king
of everything!

We'd each have a kitten,
We'd fly lots of kites,
We'd kick around balls,
and stay up most nights!

If I had a kingdom
then I would be king.
Yes, I would be king
of everything!

Betsy Franco

How People Feel About Me

My aunt says I'm perfect,
My dad says I'm great.
To grandma and grandpa,
I'm really first-rate.

They all clearly like me,
I'm sure you'll agree.
But what's most important
is that I like me.

Betsy Franco

Sometimes

Sometimes I like to be alone
And look up at the sky
And think my thoughts inside my head—
Just me, myself, and I.

Mary Ann Hoberman

Thematic Poems for the Classroom: All About Me! Scholastic Professional Books